811

THE TRACKS WE LEAVE

The Tracks

POEMS ON ENDANGERED

We Leave

WILDLIFE OF NORTH AMERICA

Barbara Helfgott Hyett

ILLUSTRATIONS BY ROBERT W. TREANOR

UNIVERSITY OF ILLINOIS PRESS   URBANA AND CHICAGO

Illustrations © 1996 by Robert W. Treanor
© 1996 by the Board of Trustees of the University of Illinois
Manufactured in the United States of America

1   2   3   4   5   C   P   5   4   3   2   1

This book is printed on acid-free paper.

Library of Congress Cataloging-in-Publication Data
Hyett, Barbara Helfgott.
The tracks we leave : poems on endangered wildlife of North
    America / Barbara Helfgott Hyett ; Illustrations by Robert W.
    Treanor.
p.   cm.
ISBN 0-252-02235-1 (cloth : alk. paper). — ISBN 0-252-06575-1
    (pbk. : alk. paper)
1. Endangered species—North America—Poetry. 2. Rare
    animals—North America—Poetry. 3. Zoology—North
    America—Poetry.
I. Title.
PS3558.E4744T73   1996
811'.54—dc20   95-41830
                    CIP

For my sons, Eric and Brian,
who keep watch

ACKNOWLEDGMENTS

I am grateful to the Massachusetts Cultural Council and the Brookline Council on the Arts and Humanities for grants that enabled me to travel to wildlife sanctuaries across the country to see the species I was studying; to the Corporation at Yaddo, the Virginia Center for the Creative Arts, and the Helene Wurlitzer Foundation of New Mexico for fellowships that let me live and write in settings rare enough to inspire poems; to the U.S. Department of Wildlife and Fisheries, the National Wildlife Fund, the Museum of Science, Boston, and the California Academy of Sciences for research assistance; to the Writer's Room of Boston, Inc., haven at which I both conceived and completed the book; to Mag Dimond, Orlando Salazar, and Linda Swindle for settling me into Taos; to Cal Zabarsky, who exhibited the family ferrets; to Marvin Hyett, who repeatedly sent me prints of his eloquent wildlife work; to my beloved poet-friends who read and read these poems; to Liz Dulany, at the University of Illinois Press, for encouraging me from the start and for seeing the book through; and especially to my husband, Norman, for sustaining me during the difficult years of the work.

Several poems, some under different titles, some in earlier forms, have appeared in the following publications:

Agni Review: "Gray Bat," "Roseate Tern"; *College English:* "Schaus Swallowtail Butterfly," "we've walked for hours"; *Hampden-Sydney Review:* "American Crocodile"; *Hudson Review:* "In the Presence of Snakes"; *Kalliope:* "American Burying Beetle"; *New Republic:* "Atlantic Ridley Sea Turtle"; *Partisan Review:* "Northern Swift Fox"; *Prairie Schooner:* "American Alligator," "Houston Toad," "North American Ridge-Nosed Rattlesnake"; *Salamander:* "Grizzly Bear"; *Sing Heavenly Muse!:* "Florida Panther," "Giant Kangaroo Rat"; *Southern Poetry Review:* "Texas Blind Salamander"; *Stuff Magazine:* "let any bee fly into the kitchen"; *Women's Review of Books:* "I have seen you wrestle a fishhook," "in the meadow that skirts the mountain"; *Yankee:* "Bald Eagle."

ILLUSTRATOR'S NOTE

In 1974 Barbara Helfgott Hyett saw some of my ink line drawings of animals and spoke with enthusiasm about subject and technique. Four years ago I told her about my ink wash painting of a kangaroo rat and Barbara told me she had just completed a poem about the same animal. That coincidence led to our collaboration on *The Tracks We Leave*.

In these paintings, I have used an ink and watercolor wash that insists upon a rapid and fluid response to the nature of the subject. The washes are layered to suggest color and pattern as well as the textures of fur, feathers, scales, and hair. A few paintings are worked into with conte crayon and pastel in the last layer. In these personal images, I wanted to convey the movement and grace, the strength and frailty, but mostly the courage of each of these creatures as it fights to sustain itself in our times.

CONTENTS

BECAUSE

> . . . *because everything here*
> *apparently needs us, this fleeting world, which in some strange way*
> *keeps calling to us. Us, the most fleeting of all.*
> *Once for each thing. Just once; no more. And we too,*
> *just once. And never again.*
> —Rainer Maria Rilke, *The Ninth Elegy*

Deep within a cave on the Edwards plateau, halfway between Austin and San Antonio, the Texas blind salamander burrows in mold. There is only one entrance to its habitat; I sat there for hours, waiting, hoping to see for myself that pale transparent body, the red burlesque of plumes. The blind salamander starts out life sighted, then staves off adulthood by going under, crawls on its larval belly into this one and only place on earth, adapts here to absolute darkness and the inky feel of subterranean cold. Refusing to metamorphose, this is a species equipped to breed without copulating, able to exist for years without food. It has established for itself a way of being that it has followed since the Pliocene, depending as we do on water, which flows constantly in and out of its body, on gravity, and on the sturdiness of earth's sustaining crust.

The Tracks We Leave expresses the ingenious and boisterous lives of thirty-eight North American creatures whose names appear, or once did, on the U.S. Department of Wildlife and Fisheries's Endangered and Threatened Wildlife List. The poems represent each official category: mammal, bird, reptile, amphibian, fish, mollusc, crustacean, insect, and arachnid. I have also included poems of my own encounters with the wild. Each of the latter charts my journey through the ordinary thicket of life and death: I came upon a dead deer, an elk rotting, a dog stuffed into a bag, a stiff parakeet on my windowsill; I witnessed the mating of black snakes, studied my husband as he fed melon to a monarch butterfly, carried an injured gull in my arms. In the Hasidic tradition, the creation of the world ends with God's smashing of the vessel of life; from there it is the responsibility of each person to restore the shards.

I portray creatures not as they are perishing but as they are persisting. Their circumstances are precarious—like ours. In a 1992 study of the status of earth's living resources, the World Conservation Monitoring Center ranked the United States first in the world for its number of threatened reptiles, amphibians, and fishes and tenth for its threatened birds. In 1995 the U.S. Department of Wildlife and Fisheries listed 325 endangered and 111 threatened species in North America alone. No listed species has been restored to truly sustainable numbers. Making the list in the first place is a signal of doom. And how many unlisted creatures will become extinct? It is not mine to tell how the human species is dependent upon the survival of creatures in the wild, though surely this is so.

I don't remember exactly when I began to pay attention to the newt on the wall of my son's fish tank or to activity at the bird feeder or to the interesting sleeping behavior of my cat. In that watchful mind I happened upon the clacking of thirty horseshoe crabs mating in a tidepool at a marsh. Amazed by the frenzy, I crouched beside them, tried to comprehend what I was seeing. Afterwards, I read about the process in the encyclopedia, learned the facts. Here was a poet's trove, a lexicon I'd never known.

I prescribed for myself a course of study; first, reading: all of the classical natural histories. In *De Anima*, Aristotle wonders: *"If what exists is not a plurality of souls but a plurality of parts of one soul, which ought we to investigate first, the whole soul or its parts?"* I was coming to imagine a project, a collection of wildlife poems that might speak to the concerns of a world trembling, unstable at the turn of a new century. I read Ptolemy and Pliny, Lamarck's *Zoological Philosophy*, Thoreau and Emerson, the theories of Darwin and Lorenz. I discovered the syntax of animal behaviorists: Huxley on crayfish, Maeterlinck on bees, Fabre on insect worlds, and soon I was shopping in the wildlife section of bookstores—buying contemporary works by Barry Lopez, Diane Ackerman, Peter

Matthiessen, and Roger Caras and the photographs of Susan Mitchell. I found a copy of the 1973 Endangered Wildlife Act and wrote the U.S. Department of Wildlife and Fisheries for the most recent list of endangered and threatened species. Stunned by the inordinate length of that list, I decided to write poems about the creatures whose names appeared there, irresistible names—*American burying beetle, Appalachian monkey-face pearly mussel*—until *blue whale, peregrine falcon, grizzly bear* became equally crucial to me. Everyone was clamoring to be let in.

I began with Huxley's common crayfish, found myself drawn to unpopular creatures: salamanders and alligators, rats, mice, toads. I learned how amphibians dig or breathe, how they exchange gases just beneath the skin. Often, I caught myself reciting, under my breath, a line from Mary Oliver's "The Kitten": *"This is real."* Wanting so much to resist anthropomorphic analysis, I worked hard to regard the creatures accurately. I was stunned by the predicament each one embraced in its particular niche—blind or earless or holding to the barest branch. I was becoming morally bound to the creatures I was trying to describe, feeling a personal obligation to explicate them, for their sake and for mine.

Five years passed. The American alligator was removed from the endangered species list; the northern spotted owl was added. Species not yet listed were disappearing. I decided to travel to wildlife sanctuaries across the country, to swamps and deserts and mountains of old-growth forests, hoping to glimpse what, until then, only photographs and drawings told. The first endangered creature I actually saw—sunning itself against mangrove roots in the Bailey tract in Sanibel, Florida—was an American alligator. The following Christmas, I rented a canoe and paddled through the Everglades until I looked into the face of a manatee. In J. M. "Ding" Darling National Wildlife Refuge, not even seeking a sighting, I stood transfixed before an eleven-foot-long American crocodile; no more than two feet ahead of me, she yawned. At Ballard Locks in Washington State, I watched—unbelievably—one single sockeye salmon, far too small, swim alone against the tide. And on the prairie in New Mexico, I stopped my friend from driving on and got out of the car as an unwary pronghorn walked beside the passenger door—too close. She stood beside us, breathing, then ran in a wide circle, as if she meant to show us the splay and dazzle of her white fur rump.

Throughout my travels, I was the eager trespasser, uneasy in the wild. At Ruby Beach, on the Olympic Peninsula, an eagle cried, swooped at me from a nest in a Douglas fir, warning me away. I had to hike farther and farther into forests of the Cascade Mountains to glimpse if not the northern spotted owl itself then at least the roots and stones it had stood on. Most of the animals depicted in this collection have been endangered by loss of habitat, pushed into smaller and smaller confines by wetland condos, trailer parks, tracts of single-family houses. Some individuals were poisoned: DDT made the shells of eggs too brittle to be sat upon by brooding eagles; chemistry was depleting rivers and salmon and mussels of oxygen itself. The very fabric of American commerce is pushing wildlife to the brink. Some creatures are inching back. The status of bald eagles has been upgraded from endangered to threatened. But in April, at Riverbanks Zoo in Columbia, South Carolina, I stood beside one languishing, some of its down caught in the chain links of its cage. In Ipswich, Massachusetts, I sat on a bench outside a backyard fence in the presence of a family of gray wolves and the human couple who keeps them. And while gray wolves are increasing in number, one alpha male released by federal authorities into Idaho this winter has already been found shot dead, the government-issued banding collar neatly laid out in the grass beside him. Is it possible to balance the undoing, to exact the sorrow and the shame?

In 1985, when I was completing my second collection of poetry, *Natural Law*, I read in the newspaper that there were five dusky seaside sparrows left on earth. Living in captivity, in Florida, they were all males, the remnant of their kind. Because these were the birds that filled the Atlantic coast in my girlhood, I wrote them into a small poem. By the following year, there were only two. On June 16, 1987, in an aviary in Disney World, the last dusky seaside sparrow fell dead. Nature is not the pure and separate nation I had once imagined. I cannot save anything but with words.

Shot from the bow of his insistence,
flung into sunlight with a sound
like tearing silk, he touches her
mouth with his head. Her tongue is
flicking. Already she moves away.

Now they work their heads like two
stones sparking, his length climbing
the stairs of her, sliding up until even
the thin tips of their tails are twining,
untwining. He is thumping upon her
to be let in.

He lifts himself from her body
and in that blackness his penis
appears, everted, unlidded, pink
as the underpetals of a rose,
the foam of his being pouring
from him into less and less.

They rest, coiled on one another,
her head lifted as a Sphinx.
They are wrapped in quiet
breathing. They are snakes.

In the grass, they wind toward
the hollow of a tree; the starlings
startled, flying outward one by one.
This is the graspable Eden, requited
in all of its urgings: Life declaring itself
in opposition—*For me! For me!*

THE TRACKS WE LEAVE

in the woods where I am, rain
falls with a deep-green sound.
I have tracked a fox,
witnessed a blue heron
balance on a branch
as if stillness
were easy

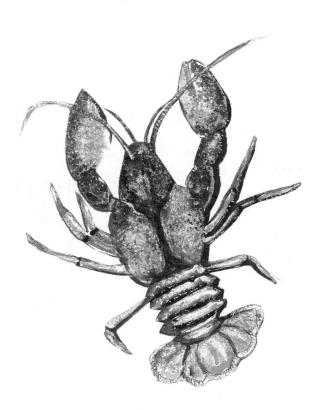

CAVE CRAYFISH

—Cambras zophonastes

At noon she walks the bottom
of the shallows, a hungry engine,
feeding on the poisoned and the drowned.
Her gills are delicate plumes.
Like lariats, feelers whip, propelled
by a wide, hexagonal heart.

She outgrows her carapace:
Black pyramidal eyes are first to withdraw.
Then legs, four crazy pairs squeezing
through. Whatever rips off is left
behind; the sheath gives way to body—
soft, dark brown as earth. Naked beside
her harder self, one is the crayfish,
the other, her hollow twin.

SCHAUS SWALLOWTAIL BUTTERFLY

—Papilio aristodemus ponceanus

By true and false legs, a larva
holds tightly to thistle, wild
cherry, phlox, disguised as a leaf,
shedding its skin five times.

It lives to eat; pulsed to the limit
of accumulation. It cannot stop
the crunch and pause of feeding—
thirteen walking segments, a mouth
for chewing, spoon-shaped jaws.

Sexless, it comprehends
the sexual language
of the elements—sun passing
through the gates of cuticle,
entering the body, absorbed.

Full and complete in its final assemblage,
it wanders, aimless across fields; stops;
binds its tail by a silken girdle
to a twig. It will give up the glut,
replacing itself, indulging
the adult it must become.

ATLANTIC RIDLEY SEA TURTLE

—Lepidochelys kempii

In the give and take of water, she swims
with sharks, jawfish, limbs arcing, birdlike,
pressing an ocean back over the axis
of her spine. She emerges loudly. Sunlight
erupting from her shell, she glances
sideways, over the green light of land, climbs
the colossal dunes. Above the reach of tides
she curls her forelimb inward: shoveling
her shadow out of sand. She lays
her eggs two at a time. For hours.

The descent to the sea is the darkness
she was born to, hatched first and waiting,
passive beneath one hundred of her
hatchling kind—shells breaking,
caving the roof and walls; bodies
wet and scrambling, sands falling,
the floor rising; the whole nest
quaking in that first disorder.

as I stand on the sodden moss
banking the pond, a snapping turtle
swims past four ducklings, snatches
the mother, drags her by a leg
to the far shore, her wings lifting,
wings slapping the water down.
And at my feet, swallowtails
fallen from the sky. Black dust
tinges the insides of my fingers
as I touch the wings, fold them
into my handkerchief, walk on

AMERICAN CROCODILE

—Crocodylus acutus

Even before she slits the egg she is
groaning, taking on vegetable heat.
The leaves of the nest are rank
with decay. Coiled in the egg,
Buddha enclosed in herself,
striped yellow from eyelid to back.

Since the melt of glaciers, she has
followed the sun in its circle,
unable to turn around.

At the edge of water, she basks,
sliding in on her armored belly,
waving that ponderous tail.
Fed to repletion she roars,
the genius of that noise
making the surface dance.

WOOD BISON

—*Bison bison athabascae*

Bulls punish the trees, smash
their horns into saplings, spar
in a scrim of dust. They lay
outstretched, the counterpoise
of mountains. The rut builds
slowly: A male straggles in,

outweighing any female
by a thousand pounds—he swings
himself upon her, his chin a post
in her shoulder; his hooves stripping
blood from her hide.

Birthing, she flattens her body
against the solace of stones.
Licked into standing, her calves
nuzzle, all of them mooing
and bleating, the blue milk
that passes between them
so rich, one suck is enough.

AMERICAN PEREGRINE FALCON

—Falco peregrinus anatum

The tercel transports meat
in his yellow talons. His mate
has disappeared into air.
Braced on the edge of the eyrie,
the fledglings preen.

So soon from the egg, they lack
the impulse to harness the rising
spiral; swoop in play—wings folded
in against the body's precipitate
dive, each head crooked into its own

black helmet. Flight is their chisel
and their hammer; and though the sky
is free and wheeling, they hold to cliffs.
At night they roost near one another,
on separate ledges in the dark.

where train tracks cross
the valley, a deer lying sideways
in a gully, muzzle barely grazing
grass. I crouch to watch: The left flank
is torn and eaten—no flies bother
that empty cage. The body lies
compliant, hooves pointed
as in dance. Death is tenacious
beside the road, one small mouth
stiffening into thrust. Blood
mottles the flesh beneath an open
eye, not gruesome, but shining
with a steadiness I've never known

KEY DEER

—Odocoileus virginianus clavium

Toughening begins at conception—
she grows durable, surviving drought,
the misery of summer flies

that hatch in her nasal chambers,
her mouth; they penetrate her hide.
She looks only forward, or to the sides

where everything is forb and succulence.
When she comes into heat, she douses
the woods with scent concealed in the orbits

of her eyes. Shadows materialize;
she glides out of the mangroves, looks
over her shoulder, ears pressed to the trail.

She teaches her young by example:
when to stand still at the edge
of watching; when to run.

GRAY BAT

—Myotis grisescens

Born in synchrony, the infants gasp,
emerge blind from bodies hanging
by thumbs. They suckle in absolute
darkness, cradled in tails, mothers
licking their leathery wings.

They are modest as lichens,
meticulous, always combing, pink
tongues oiling their claws. Sinewy-
shouldered, slender-hipped, they sleep
through winter, vulnerable in their coma,
the caves they inhabit not hidden enough.
When they wake they warm themselves—
even in fur they must shiver before they can fly.

At night they hunt by galactic sound—
calls pulsed from the nose, vibrating
every airy recess, releasing
the solid shape of things.

thunder, and the magpies break
into screaming. The sun still falls
onto the peaked horizon, staining
the great geometry of mountains
blood-red. I want to stay forever
beside the river, so strong it sluices
rock face. I want to occupy that surge.
Everything is changing—the rain's
bel canto, the chromatic sky. Night
has yet to take the blaze away

BALD EAGLE

—Haliaeetus leucocephalus

Architect of twigs and sorrow,
she nests in the oldest forests
below the tops of dying trees;
most of the eggs too soft to survive.

Still, she builds up a brooding basket
decorated with a spray of pine.
In the egg cup, moss-mounds, feathers,
the heads of fish.

Crouched on the branch,
conspicuous, she patiently eyes
the ocean that flows deftly
beneath her, the wide open wind.

Born crying, an eaglet pips a hole
in the brittleness around it. Stripped
of its shell, it feeds and it feeds,
asks for nothing more.

CALIFORNIA BROWN PELICAN

—Pelecanus occidentalis californicus

From adults she has learned
ingratiation, helped them feed her
elder nestling, stave off the thirst
for blood. She has brooded fiercely,
rebuilding the nest the tides have
battered for forty million years.

She lives by pausing above a school
of fish, knows where to plunge
and just how deeply. At the edge
of the ocean's tenancy, she obeys
the flock. If gulls must torment
she lets them, flies among them,
wears one as a fetish on her brow.

She is the soul of the species,
a heavy creature, mute but for the heart.

NEW MEXICAN RIDGE-NOSED RATTLESNAKE

—Crotalus willardi obscurus

The face of the snake mirrors the earth
she crawls on: canyons sunk below
the nostrils; a precipice risen on the snout;
all of her life, lengthening, rattling
the end of her tail. She rests, head still
at the center of the circle.

Her listless eyes turn blue
as nursing milk, the scab of her skin
loosening in the eyecap, splitting
the corners of the mouth: drawn
back against rock, against thistle —
rubbed off, abandoned inside-out.

let any bee fly into the kitchen,
and you will stop it in a glass
atop a saucer, shake it safely
out the window, into a world
you believe in. You love to
fish with homemade lures
at any shoreline; but not until
the lip of a keeper bass is hooked
and bleeding do you let it go.
And when a bat comes
streaking through our living
room, you snare it with a net,
bring it down, splay the amazing
hands to show me, hurting
the thing you mean so hard to know

HOUSTON TOAD

—Bufo houstonensis

She comes out in rain, listens to insects hum
even after sound has ceased; the degenerate
eyes fired by what moves at dusk: moth,
beetle, peripatetic wing. Stomach
contracting, she feeds, tongue
snapping up a parliament of flies.

Eyes closed, she eats her own skin whole.
In the underskin, she races against drying,
burrows into soil, needing to feel
the hard sides of things, all day
immobile, disguised as stone.

At the breeding pond, the males sing; first
in creation to sing, before birds, the voice
ventriloquial, loud. All night, this instinct—
even underwater, nostrils closed, they trill.
In resolute silence she chooses one
dark throat, follows it into the grasses
until she touches that sound.

AMERICAN ALLIGATOR

—Alligator mississippiensis

They seek one another in the sedges,
veil the Everglades in undeciphered perfume.
They bellow loudly for days.

When she moves to deep water he follows;
when she climbs onto land, he lies
beside her on the bare bank, stroking
her back with his hand.

He mounts her in shallow water,
head seeking the sensitive margin
of her mouth; rubs her throat
with the scutes of his neck, grasping
her neck with his jaws. He bends
beneath her the thick wallet of his tail.

Everything wavers: shadows
on their delicate eyeballs, the lids
of their ears, their inner ears,
ten thousand vibrating hairs—
the sun trembling as it enters
the slits of their eyes.

FLORIDA PANTHER

—Felis concolor coryi

High-browed, slim as a cypress,
starving, not born to the swamp
but forced to live there, she's still
seeking a prairie's wide ground.
Mosquitoes torment her small ears.

Alone in her season, she cries,
that vessel ascending the mangroves.
A male arrives; his body, a panoply
of scars. He plays at biting her, jumps
cautiously aside.

For a week they hunt together,
barely parting the tips of grasses.
Theirs is a subtle wildness. For
a week they sleep in the open,
untrusting, side by side.

every bookshelf holds your trophies—
conchs, lichens, a pair of Rhinoceros beetles,
one vertebra of a humpback whale.
We read about the mating habits
of crocodiles, spend days in a canoe
in the Everglades, searching rivers
for a pair of manatees, find them
rolling, brushing against each other
muscular lips. I used to be afraid
of pigeons; now I keep snakeskins, brittle
carapaces horseshoe crabs outgrow.
From you I've learned the silent love
that creatures sign by touching
flippers, the scutes of throats

MANATEE

—Trichechus manatus

Born underwater, she mates
underwater, flippers clasped
in unembarrassed need. At night
she swims through green ribbons
of water hyacinths, her tail streaking
the bottom with mythic circles,
an alphabet in mud and slime.

Everything about her is articulate:
snout bristles, nostrils that close
and open, every fine hair
on the wrinkled skin.

Grounded in water, she is massive,
the fulcrum of plentitude;
suspended in sleep she will break
the crystalline surface to breathe.
Life is divisive—the body
keeps her world from being whole.

WHOOPING CRANE

—Grus americana

She stands in the ambiguity of mudflats
on one leg, without trembling, the tallest
bird. Her feathers have weathered

whitely. The red skin of her forehead
is bared like fire. Far and farther
are the zones of her existence.

She knows what she needs and how
to get it, strides stately through
any school of fish, dipping, seizing

from their hollows, tender crabs.
Song is coiled like an umbilicus in her
windpipe. She answers her mate

with a higher call. He whoops.
She whoops, her long back sloping.
He bows, leaps, throws his face

to the sky. She prances. They arch
their necks, bend themselves, jump
into air together. Earth is the anchor.

They run, wings opened
to one another, prolonging the dance—
more leaping, more elegant bows.

behind the house you dig
a winter grave, stony earth
yielding until your shovel finds
the roots of the hardest tree—
black walnut—on which to lay
her body down: the housecat,
Karma. I'd restrained her
on my lap, petted her face
while the vet injected poison,
unwiring the cortex first,
then her heart, grayed fur
uncannily gleaming, eyes stunned
open, perfectly green; her body
reforming in its afterlife, arched
against the betrayal of my hand

GRIZZLY BEAR

—Ursus arctos

Lethargy settles into her heartbeat
as she moves to her den hours before
the storm. The disc of her face
is an ancient god. Asleep, her body
curves inward to feed: fat berries,
fish, mice, flesh of violets, a thicket
of purple stars.

Spring is riddled with torment.
The cubs suck her roughly:
Her teats are scratched, bitten raw.
The young play, parry like boxers
and she is their watcher,
as nervous as water, as kind.

ROSEATE TERN

—Sterna dougalli

Drifting sideways before a heavy rain,
they blush like the inside of shells.
In the mating strut, they lock bills,
droop the pointed wings. He stands
on her back, tail streaming like ribbons.
When they are done they coo.

They are all laying, some at the roots
of the tallest grasses, some on stones.
They nest among vines of poison ivy;
the male is a shield against the sun.
The hatchlings run as soon as
the shell is cast.

Now the sky is a horde of terns diving
and every throat vibrates with a scream.
The flocks come in, fish flapping
in their beaks, each bird searching
for its own seed among the multitude,
smelling the hunger of the young.

I have seen you wrestle a fishhook
from the mouth of a cormorant. Hip deep
in water, you straddled wings, unraveled
filament to set them free. You can hear
the hurt of birds, have rescued one gull
after another found sitting too tamely on sand.
I've helped you carry a black-back to the car.
Swaddled in your shirt it accepted the human
restraint of your arms. You drove to the refuge.
In the backseat I sat still, holding the hollow
wand of its wing. I tried to keep the face
covered on my lap, but the beak got out,
whipped against my thigh. Fearing that
otherness, I remembered a lullaby, sang

BLUE WHALE

—Balaenoptera musculus

Only the dorsal fin is comprehensible,
life-size, as she dives, leaving a liquid
footprint, smoothing over the places
she has been. In the valley of magnetism
all roads are invisible; yet she follows
them, her ear a simple window.

Her body is a second self, the tutelary
angel whose speech is a form of dreaming.
The lens of her eye is crystal. Her protector
is tears. She can close herself off
when she wants to: blowhole and glottis;
each bronchus with a sphincter all its own.

In the breach between real and unfathomed
breath is an act of devotion: If she beaches,
her heft will crush her. Confined to existence,
she is driven from pole to pole, by ice
to warmth, and back to ice again.

SONORAN PRONGHORN

—Antilocapra americana sonoriensis

Native of an ancient family, the one
survivor of her tribe is too fast
for coyotes, too strong.

Blizzards drift before her; sagebrush
pads the fences she must crawl
under, or through. She belongs

to the treeless open, canvassing
great distances to make herself
secure. The split hearts of her

soles are senseless. She doesn't
feel the ground. The oversized lungs
are greedy. She runs, mouth open,

leaning inward, head high, racing
in circles, widening the rim
of the decimated carousel.

GIANT KANGAROO RAT

—Dipodymys ingens

Against the wall of her burrow,
huge hindfeet drum, that vast
persistence as hollow
as oceans about to be filled.

Life is patient within her.
She waits out the desert
sun; emerges under cool
night stars, afraid of rain
and any trace of moonlight.

In the absence of shadows,
she goes lightly, gathering
fruits of whatever roots
are there, packing the pouches
of fur-lined cheeks.

Almost holy, she does not
drink but thrives on seeds
her body's alchemy
turns into wine.

now I watch you, intent
in a canvas beachchair, feeding
melon to a butterfly, proboscis
lapping juice from the reservoir
of your thumb. A monarch
entrusting itself to your body—
when you first crouched down,
it stepped onto your finger,
one wing torn useless, scales
paling, one wing beating itself
against the back of your hand.
You placed it on your shoulder
and it clung there, thirsting
beside the sea for miles

SOCKEYE SALMON

—Onchorhynchus nerka

Salmon hatch strong, perceiving pain
from the start—the weight of water,
air penetrating the skin of nerves.
Without eyelids they do not sleep
but float to the ocean, listless, growing
old slowly, scales seasoned with rings.

They return to spawn. No one knows
how they find the mouth of that river:
ascending the stairs of perseverance,
smelling the streams they were born in,
fighting rapids, leaping the waterfall.

Exhausted, they spill upon the riverbank,
smashing their skulls on rocks
and dying or, stunned, struggling
back to water again, leaping again,
out of their element, bruised
bodies turned into wheels.

WOODLAND CARIBOU

—Rangifer tarandus caribou

She has kept her summer antlers,
rid of velvet. Such bare grace
she wields as a weapon, butting
naked bulls away.

What is hers comes in winter—
a sufficiency of lichens
easily released of snow.

Her eyes enlarge the darkness.
She is nothing
that does not reach or bend.

The earth turns to receive
each footfall, the pads of her hooves
hardening, cutting the tundric ice.

Within her heels, small bones click.
The tendons in her ankles slide
into music when she runs.

TOOTH CAVE SPIDER

—Leptoneta myopica

Pale and freshly molted
from her instar, blood runs
blue through the book
of her lungs, her small
encumberances: eight
jointed legs and the hairs
upon them, short-sighted
rows of simple eyes.

She can feel any pulse
struggling through
rooms she has walled
off in thin air. She feeds
from within that tangle,
bending her head to
free the fangs.

Persistent as a scar
turned white in healing,
she shoots through
the spigot of her body
silk she can stand on:
Without wings, without
gossamer or shadow,
she clings by a claw
to that swaying bridge.

we've walked for hours beside the river
when a shadow sweeps in: "Black-crowned
night heron" you say as it lands
on the branch beside you. Another, and soon,
incredibly, a flock substantiates the tree.
Did you call them to you? People stare.
You are not surprised, watching birds
calm themselves, perched and staying

NORTHERN SWIFT FOX

—Vulpes velox hebes

She circles into wind, lies down,
reconsiders the trail on which
she's come. Danger flattens
the black ears against her.
Fur is a batting of stars.

At night, she discovers every cache
she has hidden, unburying the flesh
and the bones: What will be eaten,
what carried away in a life
without malice or shame?

Compelled to pursue the shoulders
of a fat mouse, a rabbit's neck,
she must stalk again. Behind her
eyes are mirrors. She can see
herself in the famine between kills.

BLACK-FOOTED FERRET

—Mustela nigripes

Thief of darkness, her body
is low-slung, swaybacked, a gently
rolling plain. Made of motion
she's a silent factory, perfect
listener, a flexible agile mind.
Courage impells her into burrows,
untamping the plugs of tunnels, taking
for her own the prairie dog's town.

The life she assumes is a hidden
one, her gait bent and worried,
her fur, pale honey in the grass.
Faithful to earth, she is short-legged,
polishing the ground with the bevel
of her chin. Up on her haunches,
her neck is pliable and long.
Penumbral, she looks out, over
the landscape, projecting herself
into that black-masked equipoise.

JAGUAR

—Panthera onca

Born blind in a thicket of thorns
she remains elemental, gliding
through twilight, the mind
of that sleek body self-aware.

Peaceable, she doesn't fight
her kind but hunts alone,
in darkness, the cushion of paw
furred on the ground. She coughs

to startle a deer into disclosure,
pursues him through a forest,
tricks him, waits on a branch
to drop down—one bite

at his nape drives canines
into hindbrain, snapping
the cord. With mercy, she releases
what she's come for, into death.

By day she enjoys earthy pleasures,
emits ambrosial odor, swims for hours.
The pattern of her being is repeated
in circles: eyes in their open

orbits, the widening jaw. Eloquence
lopes along her coat's tawny territory
and a chain of spots encoding
the authority of her spine.

in the meadow that skirts the mountain,
striped underwings of vultures rise.
And here is an elk—the mutilated
carcass: Both sockets have been emptied
of eyes. The fur is as tawny as the earth
I stand on and the flies that harvest it
are blue, iridescent as sequins, clambering
in and out of the hole a bullet blew out
of its side. The rump is gone
and I see the bloated anarchy
of organs: untwined intestines,
the bloodless stomach almost floating.
What was contained is now distended—
the flags of the entrails wave.
Splayed on the grass, three of the legs
lie neatly; the fourth, taken, so precisely
severed it's hard to imagine the fall

UTAH PRAIRIE DOG

—Cybomys parvidens

Hers is a call of pleasure in abundant
grasslands, high-pitched and contagious.
Standing on her mound, she will kiss
each prairie dog who passes, not in

mating, but in the passion of familiars.
She keeps watch when it is her turn to
until danger sets her shrieking,
the two-toned whistle lapsing into

silence as the shadow of an eagle
darkens the town. For half the day
she mines tunnels, brings up undersoil,
weathers the land. She builds listening

chambers, vestibules, ramps, a room
for resting, bedded in leaves. All night
in the communal burrow she is safe
among her white-tailed coterie, her clan.

GRAY WOLF

—Canis lupus

They do not wander but know,
all of them reading the map
of their single mind. If one,
out of sight and hearing, stares
at what is moving through the forest,
the others lift their heads.

Life in the pack is the life of howling
obeisance, everyone arriving
at the rendezvous, the shy, the wary,
the leader, petulant and spoiled; every
nuance is crucial in the hierarchy—

keep to the confines of the circle,
play, gather in ceremony, sing
together like friends.

Wolves dance—push, come
too close, submit, withdraw, jump
out in surprise, practicing
fear, and something like honor:

When, in fighting, one lays out
its jugular before another's teeth,
the other walks away.

stopped to study the cows, I find,
near the splintered fence, a sack.
I bend to lift it, feel the thickness,
the cold weight of the dead relaxing
into gravity. Stuffed into that canvas
crypt, the matted hindquarters
of some animal — fox, dog, I cannot
go beyond the gold fur of the tail

POINT ARENA MOUNTAIN BEAVER

—Aplodontia rufa nigra

Not a beaver, she builds no dams
against the river; nothing is diverted
in her name. Far from the range
of mountains, she lives sequestered

in labyrinthine burrows, her work
marked by earth mounded into fans.
She prowls the path of wet grasses,
fern fronds, her five-toed hindprints

overlapping smaller foreprints as she
steps into the place she's already been.
The teeth she grows are a conundrum:
rubbed down as fast as they can rise.

She gnaws on the bark of pines, climbs
to trim off twigs and needles, leaves
as a ladder each branch's stub. See
her ascending, descending, in dark

ancestral robes, headfirst, clutching
a diadem of green wood with a paw.
She enlarges the world by going
under, digging with the force

of anonymity, her bristled body building
shrines to every stone or chunk
of clay she encounters: inclusive,
ignoring nothing, leaving nothing out.

NORTHERN SPOTTED OWL

—Strix occidentalis caurina

She sleeps all day, taunted by crows, mobbed
by the tiniest sparrows, and holds to that
branch, eight talons tucked beneath her.
She tempers her power, tamps threat

into sexual fire, screams in courtship,
mates on the knife-edge, doesn't build
but steals nests from treetops, from the gaping
stump's heart. Her eggs are hard.

Night unravels slights and ruses;
woodrats rustle the leaf-litter—*crush
the skull   undercut the belly
swallow it whole!*

She is mind incarnate: cerebrum,
cerebellum, medulla oblongata, dark
eyes that see too far. She's the fallen angel
at the lip of the timberland; her breast

is as dappled as bark. Hurled from the story,
she scans the cold mechanics of the mountain,
the river's alluvium, the falls and its deception—
the once and broken covenant of fir.

before dawn we board the Jonesport boat
in the harbor. We are cold; shiver shoulder
to shoulder as the captain's wife steers us
out of sight of land. Here is the fictive flex
of eagles, an arch of gray seals so close
we could touch them; whale after whale
risen before our eyes. Exuberant,
my husband scans the waves, pointing
with his binoculars, shouting, Minke! Finback!
I bury my hands in my sleeves. The island
is bedrock, seaweed that clambers as we do
over a bluff; one son behind me, pressing
my shoulder; one son leading me by the hand.
We run through a hail of terns to the highest
lean-to. In silence we enter the blind. Sky
seeps in between timbers. We open the four
square windows—one thousand puffins
staring in. They do not see us as we are,
hidden before them, every one of them
busy with its living, standing precariously
on orange feet. Auks cluster on a precipice.
Some are moaning, and we moan, trying
to capture that deep, inhuman sound.
We canvass the barren pallet
of their predicament—jagged granite
boulders, unforgiving, violent like first
earth. We cannot get enough of this
inclusion, loud and bold and genderless—
the reek of fish and isolation, the kinship
we are hungry for, the each to each

87

HAWAIIAN MONK SEAL

—Monachus schauinslandi

She swam the whole earth through
long-gone seaways; now she dwells among
atolls and cloistered palms, confined to
storm-swept inlets, the waters preyed by sharks.

Life restricts her to a diet of aggression
and the smallest clams. For this she is muzzle
and rooting muscle, lips to suck flesh from shells.
She gives herself to water: inside her

body, movement, fluids agitating even her
remotest nerves. At sea, it's her voice
that makes males bark. Menaced, the embryo
waits months to plant itself in that capacious

womb. Everything is submerged in her:
hindlegs bound to the pelvis, steering flipper
buried to the base of her hand. Her blood.
Her breath. All of it working to keep her down.

On the land she is tied to, she's bounty, banished
to noise and intrusion. Without sanctuary,
she swims to exhaustion, a relict species,
unwilling to learn the preserving power of fear.

SALT MARSH HARVEST MOUSE

— *Reithrodontomys raviventris*

Instrument of earth's diversion, she
is comely, consequential, a little island
embedded in reeds. Oblivious to gravity,
she can fall off a hillside, survive the shock
of landing. All winter, she swims, or floats,
on the surface of San Francisco Bay;
but her nest is grounded, a fist of grasses,
its round opening ingeniously kept closed.
Her eyes are a cosmos charged with feeling.
She obeys the laws embedded in her gums:
Drink salt. Gnaw forever, teeth perpetually
replacing whatever hunger takes away.
Night gives her dimension. Her shadow
is a seed, heaving. She hardly exists at all.

once, I watched a parakeet
feeding beside the host
of pigeons in the Public Garden;
pecking, bobbing amongst the others
like so many corks. Impossibly I saw it
again, hours later, on the ledge
of my office window, lying out there.
All winter that body surprised me.
I suppose flesh withered beneath
the surface of those wings,
but the feathers held, stayed
past their season, green

APPALACHIAN MONKEYFACE PEARLY MUSSEL

—Quadrula sparsa

Unrooted, she can extend her only foot
in any new direction, let go of tethers,
swing free. She accepts whatever lodges
beneath her armor, turns irritation
into pearls, withdraws, snaps
the two-faced surface closed.

Within that dark, every one thing
merges into every other—the flesh
of the mantel, spines and nacre, viscera
that lean into the velvet curtain of gills
where she places her eggs; she bathes them
in open water, washes upon them

the kindling ebullience of sperm.
Her body is its own betrayal: Larva hatch
in humble chambers swollen
with the thousand shining pebbles
of her brood. And when it's time,
she expels them, tiny hooks

reaching for a fish's jellied tail.
Most fall away. But some clamp down,
burrow between scales. They suck blood
parasitically for weeks, grow heavy, drop off:
Clutching the bottom by a byssus of thread,
they bind themselves to the barrio of shells.

TEXAS BLIND SALAMANDER

—Typhlomolge rathbuni

At birth she could see light bend
the horizon. She clung to the visible,
then crawled into the sensuous musk
of a cave. Now she can't see herself—
heart showing darkly through skin,
eyeballs sunk through flesh into
useless dots. In the rough escarpment
of Purgatory Creek she lives her life
in limestone, earth between her toes.
Whatever turns her flat face
from one side to the other, tracking
the flesh she feeds on, turns it upward,
as if there were someplace else to go.

life marks its equations
on the hillside; the fields are
opening and closing. And who
is to say what will become of
fireflies breathing across
the closest pasture — a wall
of stars rising from the trees,
the sky accessible, moving
downward? These dots
and flashes toward the end
of twilight are the constant
everything obeys

DUSKY SEASIDE SPARROW

—Ammospiza maritima nigrescens

Search the corners of the cage: Begin with
the splinters of the perch. Let sparrow register
itself unseen in the remotest neuron of your
brain. Does it blink? Does it balance, or fall,
that gray weight through the necessary nothing
of air? It might be looking, as we do, at the sea
that hums today, insistent. Pushed
to the edge, sparrow is a fleeting thing.

Ammospiza maritima nigrescens—say it:
Enunciate the imperceptible openings,
the vowels of its gout and blinded eye.
No longer shall singing be the hallmark.

This is the rainy summer of extinction
that keeps a sparrow's distance
in the cordgrass, shy and slate streaked.
Not by drowning in flood-mosquitoed waters;
not by wheels; not by wildfire; not
by the hooves of cattle ranging unaware.
The last dusky sparrow grows small and aged.
Mateless, he picks about the gravel
in an arbitrary forage, lies down
to perish in his dish.

AMERICAN BURYING BEETLE

—Nicrophorus americanus

They kill nothing, but fly to the site
at the slightest whiff of the just-dead—
one small body slipping toward
eternity, each cell giving in, the corpse
of an unfledged finch sinking inexorably,
a fraction of an inch at a time.

Beneath the carcass, a beetle pair,
on their backs, digging, twelve legs
thrust as levers, four claws shoveling
earth away. The grave fills with a body
turning to rankness, form transforming.

Beetles depend on the opening death
brings. They pull out every feather,
make flesh ripen into green.

On the altar of existence they condense
life to liquefaction. And when their larvae
waken, white and blind, they will press
palps upon them, one after another,
let them sip from that pool. Flags unfurl
from the tips of their antennae; black
bellies rasp against the crimson scarves
of wings. These are the sorcerer's markings:
death diminished, pulled out from under, undone.

CALIFORNIA CONDOR

—Gymnogyps californianus

Who comforts the Jeffrey pines
now that you are captured, every one
behind bars of cages in the outpost
of westernmost zoos? Vulture of the New World,

you used to stand on branches until late
morning, then soar in search of sun-drenched
carrion, brains ripening behind the eyes.
What use the scour and hiss of your tongue!

Once, you condensed the landscape, flapping
so thunderously earth shook. Prismic
lightning streamed from you, white
vestments undersided the ebony wings.

Your chicks hatch in incubation
chambers, where they are touched and touched
by puppets pretending to be you. Now who
will tell untainted wilderness to God?

Be yet fastidious. Bathe yourself;
rub your naked head and neck upon
the runic shreds of weeds. The century
is turning and we are *in extremis:* Open

your terrible red eyes. Cross the boundary
into blind gravity and sky;
pour us from the rough cup of your talons.
Carry us away again, sleeping.

Palladium
Alice Fulton (1986)
Selected by Mark Strand

Cities in Motion
Sylvia Moss (1987)
Selected by Derek Walcott

The Hand of God and a Few
Bright Flowers
William Olsen (1988)
Selected by David Wagoner

The Great Bird of Love
Paul Zimmer (1989)
Selected by William Stafford

Stubborn
Roland Flint (1990)
Selected by Dave Smith

The Surface
Laura Mullen (1991)
Selected by C. K. Williams

The Dig
Lynn Emanuel (1992)
Selected by Gerald Stern

My Alexandria
Mark Doty (1993)
Selected by Philip Levine

The High Road to Taos
Martin Edmunds (1994)
Selected by Donald Hall

Theater of Animals
Samn Stockwell (1995)
Selected by Louise Glück

The Broken World
Marcus Cafagña (1996)
Selected by Yusef Komunyakaa

OTHER POETRY VOLUMES

Local Men *and* Domains
James Whitehead (1987)

Her Soul beneath the Bone: Women's
Poetry on Breast Cancer
Edited by Leatrice Lifshitz (1988)

Days from a Dream Almanac
Dennis Tedlock (1990)

Working Classics: Poems on Industrial
Life
*Edited by Peter Oresick and Nicholas
Coles* (1990)

Hummers, Knucklers, and Slow Curves:
Contemporary Baseball Poems
Edited by Don Johnson (1991)

The Double Reckoning of Christopher
Columbus
Barbara Helfgott Hyett (1992)

Selected Poems
Jean Garrigue (1992)

New and Selected Poems, 1962–92
Laurence Lieberman (1993)

The Dig *and* Hotel Fiesta
Lynn Emanuel (1994)

For a Living: The Poetry of Work
*Edited by Nicholas Coles and Peter
Oresick* (1995)

The Tracks We Leave: Poems on
Endangered Wildlife of North America
(1996)
Barbara Helfgott Hyett